EXPERT PROFILES
VOLUME 6

Conversations with Influencers & Innovators

EXPERT PROFILES
VOLUME 6

Conversations with Influencers & Innovators

Featuring

Leise Jones

Manohar Lal Tandon

Matthew J. Cherney

Dr. Joe Schaefer

Don Johanson

Royalties from the Retail Sales of "Expert Profiles" are donated to Global Autism Project

AUTISM KNOWS NO BORDERS;
FORTUNATELY NEITHER DO WE.®

Global Autism Project 501(c)3, is a nonprofit organization which provides training to local individuals in evidence-based practices for individuals with autism.

Global Autism Project believes that every child has the ability to learn and their potential should not be limited by geographical bounds.

The Global Autism Project seeks to eliminate the disparity in service provision seen around the world by providing high-quality training to individuals providing services in their local community. This training is made sustainable through regular training trips and contiguous remote training.

You can learn more about Global Autism Project by visiting GlobalAutismProject.org.

Table of Contents

Breaking the Cycle of Bad Photography

Leise (pronounced Lisa) Jones is an award-winning portrait and event photographer for small business owners, nonprofit organizations, couples and families who are looking for photographs that tell their story, commemorate important days and communicate their missions. As owner of Leise Jones Photography, her approach is centered on helping people feel relaxed and comfortable being themselves in front of the camera.

Her photo brand storytelling for mission-driven companies helps businesses gain visibility and attract clients by documenting the events, activities and people that best communicate their unique value and message.

Leise does whatever it takes to support her portrait clients through the experience of being photographed so that the resulting photos are effortless, gorgeous and, most importantly, authentic.

Because she knows most people aren't automatically comfortable and authentic in front of the camera, Leise becomes a supportive teammate for each client. She's been known to bustle dresses, pin on boutonnieres, sew on a lost button and tell people, "Just be yourself, and I'll do the rest." Her clients consistently provide her with five-star reviews and describe her as honest, caring, professional and unobtrusive.

Conversation with Leise Jones

Tell us a bit about Leise Jones Photography and what you do for your clients.

Leise Jones: I own a photography business specializing in portraits and events, helping my clients show the story of their professional or personal life. Whether I'm shooting portraits or events for businesses, organizations or weddings, my work is focused on helping people feel comfortable and authentic in front of the camera. I want my clients to have excellent images, and for my business clients, that means photography to showcase their work, connect with their perspective clients and grow their business.

What specific outcomes have your clients achieved by working with you?

Leise Jones: I want to break the cycle of bad pictures. It's more of a personal outcome, particularly with portraits, but I want to end this narrative for you that you don't look good in pictures. We're going to stop saying that because now you know that you can look great in pictures. I think individuals have not only had a cycle of bad pictures but a cycle of bad experiences having their picture taken where they didn't realize, or feel they could, speak up and say, *"I don't like that,"* or *"That doesn't feel comfortable for me."* I love breaking that cycle and leaving people thinking and feeling *"Wow! That was actually really fun."*

I create a lot of storytelling photography for my corporate and small business clients too. It's usually part of a much bigger project to refresh their overall branding and website. They are going for a new look, feel and approach, which they get with really clean, crisp photos. Storytelling photography also works well on the nonprofit side because many organizations will use their photos in annual reports or fundraising appeals. That makes it easier for them to track and realize their return on investment in photography.

How do you help your clients see the business impact of using professional photography?

Leise Jones: Part of coaching my clients through the process involves explaining that, yes, people do actually look you up on LinkedIn and your profile will get more connections and engagement if you have a great picture. Your About page on your website is really important; that's where potential clients look for, and want to, see you. They want to know what you look like. They want to be able to connect with you.

If it's a nonprofit group, I spend time asking questions about their target audience, what they think that audience wants to see, and what values or characteristics they want to demonstrate through photos. For example, do they want to look approachable? Intellectual? Trustworthy? Then I help them create scenarios that we can photograph. I always work with real people. I don't work with models or hired talent. We're working with real people, clients and staff so we can set up the scenario of what it looks like, for example, when you meet with a client in the conference room. Here's how it looks when you are out fundraising or performing the service that your business provides. Basically, pushing clients to think outside the box of portraits and event photography to all the space in between. It makes such a difference when a prospective client or donor sees a real-life representation. I think that's really powerful.

Big agencies and companies can hire people to do all of this thinking for them but a lot of small businesses and nonprofits don't have the resources for that. They need to be their own creative agency and one of the benefits I can offer some insight there to help them be more effective.

What do you think is the most important question small business owners and nonprofit directors should ask when they're considering using photography to communicate their mission and message?

Leise Jones: Ask *"What are we trying to communicate by having pictures taken?"* So often I hear *"We're having this event and we want to get pictures of it,"* and when I ask a client why or how they'll be using the photos they don't have a plan for them. That's not a great way to start because it's a big investment to have a photographer cover an event, conference or fundraiser. You want to have a strategy. So, I think the most important questions to ask are *"Why are we having these pictures taken? What do we want to convey and how are we going to use them afterwards?"* Once a client has a strategy, it helps them feel more confident about the photo shoot, which ends up being more efficient and well executed. It saves everyone time and money to ask those questions upfront.

It's great that you have those upfront conversations to help your clients make the best use of their investment.

Leise Jones: I want the pictures to work and last. I want people to enjoy them. I want them to be what the client was looking for. A modern digital photographer's worst nightmare is that I give you the link to your photos, these beautiful photos that we've made and you've invested thousands of dollars in, and they sit in a folder on your computer. Make sure your pictures have a life outside of your laptop. I always get excited when I see the pictures out in their natural habitat. When I pick up a brochure and I see a picture we made, it's really exciting to know that it got used. It has a life. We want this to be a photo that is going to sing your story so let's make it good.

What are some of the common fears business owners have when it comes to getting professional headshots?

Leise Jones: Being uncomfortable and nervous in front of the camera prevents people from getting a great photo. I'm out to debunk this myth that having your picture taken is stressful and scary. The number one thing that people say is that they're not photogenic. I inherently don't believe there is such a thing as photogenic. We are not genetically predisposed to taking good pictures. I push people to not use the word photogenic because it's this mask that we put on that doesn't actually explain what is it that you don't like about how you look in pictures.

How do you help your clients break through that mental barrier?

Leise Jones: I take a counseling approach, a deep dive about your experiences being photographed, what you don't like when you look at a picture of yourself, what bothers you the most. We all have a thing, right? "*I don't like my smile and my teeth. I'm overweight and that makes me feel uncomfortable in photos.*" A lot of that we can work on through posing and lighting. These are things that we can control when we're doing a photo session.

It's a personalized and collaborative process to help get my clients comfortable in front of the camera. I help them with how to pose, where to look, what to do with their hands, whether to show their teeth or not. People start to see that just because you don't usually like how your teeth look doesn't mean you can't ever take a good picture. I am patient and I listen to my clients concerns, then offer suggestions. They have to be open to the suggestions too so I focus on building trust with them through that process and say things like "*Let's just try you sitting this way. Let's just see what it looks like. If you hate it, we'll never do it again.*" We always look at their pictures on site, which boosts their confidence and allows them to say "*I really don't like how my hair looks. Let me change it,*" or "*I don't like my glasses, let's try some without them."* Nine times out of 10 they say *"Wow! That looks really good actually."*

Do you have a specific example?

Leise Jones: I recently did 25 portraits for a college in Boston. The photos are going to be used for a staff directory and website. People were feeling nervous and would start off right away with a disclaimer. *"I have this thing on my face that I really hate. And you know, my daughter's wedding, this thing happened. And I hate how I look, I don't have enough hair up here."* People start with the things that they don't like and all that does is begin the negative self-talk. They're preparing themselves to hate how they look in the picture. I watch it happen and then I say *"You're getting in your head. Just take a deep breath. Let's just do this and look at it so we can see what you look like."* It's an amazing experience to watch people come in so nervous and certain they're going to hate how they look, then walk out feeling like they accomplished something.

What inspired you to become a photographer?

Leise Jones: Before I became a photographer, I was working as a community organizer so I come from the nonprofit sector, which definitely informs my opinions about photography for nonprofit groups. I was feeling like I wasn't having the kind of impact I wanted to have on issues that I cared about. I was feeling frustrated mostly with the politics involved in fundraising and volunteer activation. I also wanted to work for myself and be out in the world able to make something every day. I always loved photography as a hobby and thought it would be a cool career. There was a photography school in Boston so it just sort of happened, but the big factors were that I wanted to be more creative, work for myself and create a different way to interface with nonprofit organizations.

Can you share a lesson that you learned early on that still impacts how you do your business today?

Leise Jones: Early on I learned that most clients are looking for photographers who are specialists in their field. In the beginning of my career I was doing any photography; products, food, headshots, interiors. I was doing everything. Now I only photograph people, which translates to event photography and portraits. My specialty is interacting with people, helping people feel comfortable in front of the camera and helping them be themselves.

What else should people know about hiring a professional photographer?

Leise Jones: For groups or businesses thinking about hiring a photographer in conjunction with a web design project, include the web designer in the discussion about photography. Or when you're thinking about specific promotional material that you want to create, like an annual report for example, have the designer involved in the photography planning because if those people aren't involved in the planning and brainstorming about the photography piece, the photos could be wrong. They may not fit the website. They're going to have to be cropped too tight or it's the wrong orientation.

Writers too. I often ask the clients *"What's the story that's being written that this photo will accompany?"* because I want to make sure that the photo is telling the same story as the words. If they're not, you could be wasting your money because we may have to come back out and photograph this person again once you have figured out the story. Include all the creative people involved in the project in your discussions. You'll save time and money.

About Leise Jones

Since 2009, Leise Jones has specialized in making authentic, natural-looking photographs of people and events. She works with small businesses, non-profit organizations, couples and families of all kinds who are looking for photographs to tell their story, commemorate their important days and communicate their missions. Her approach to photography is centered on helping people feel comfortable enough to be themselves in front of the camera. Specializing in photo brand storytelling for mission-driven companies, she helps businesses gain visibility and attract clients by documenting the events, activities and people that best communicate their unique value and message. For wedding and portrait clients, Leise does whatever it takes to support them through the experience of being photographed so that the resulting photos are effortless, gorgeous and, most importantly, authentic.

Described by her clients as honest, caring, professional and unobtrusive, Leise has received unanimous five-star reviews on Wedding Wire and Yelp, as well as the Couples' Choice Award in 2015, 2016 and 2017. She is a member of the Professional Photographers of America, has a B.A. from Mount Holyoke College and a certificate in Professional Photography from the New England School of Photography. Leise lives in the Roslindale neighborhood of Boston with her amazing wife, hilarious twins and lazy housecats. She travels throughout New England to work on making beautiful and authentic photographs with her book of awesome clients.

WEBSITE
LeiseJones.com

EMAIL
leise@leisejones.com

LOCATION
Boston, MA

INSTAGRAM
Instagram.com/LeiseJonesPhoto

FACEBOOK
Facebook.com/LeiseJonesPhoto

TWITTER
Twitter.com/LeiseJonesPhoto

LINKEDIN
LinkedIn.com/in/LeiseJones

Generations of Continuous Innovation and Transformation

The breathtaking growth and change in the technology world over the past fifty years has touched nearly every aspect of business and daily life. In this sea of revolutionary transformation, there are few constants. Yet, Manohar Lal (M.L.) Tandon, chairman of Tandon Group, has been at the heart of the tech industry from the early days of punch cards and floppy discs, and continues to influence today's dynamic entrepreneurial community.

Throughout a career that has spanned five decades, M.L. Tandon has transformed the business community in India and around the world through technological advances, as well as social change. When he started Tandon Magnetics in the 1970s, government restrictions and cultural norms kept all female workers from working in the industry from 10 p.m. to 6 a.m., which kept many women out of the technology world. Seeing this as a lost opportunity for female workers and great loss of productivity to the nation, M.L. Tandon had the insight to see the value in a workforce of women and petitioned to have the laws changed. Later, he changed lives by offering unprecedented opportunities to women.

He was also instrumental in changing laws in India that allowed for more open trade and launching his home country into the international market.

Today, Tandon Group incubates promising startup companies and operates successful businesses in India and North America. The companies Tandon Group fosters solve significant problems in industries such as IT, healthcare, financial services and e-commerce. M.L. Tandon shares his expertise in, and influence on, industry and innovation in India, overcoming common obstacles and lessons learned through his illustrious career.

Conversation with M.L. Tandon

Tell us about Tandon Group and how the company is helping startups in India.

M.L. Tandon: Tandon Group is a technology catalyst that owns several successful businesses. We provide resources to next-generation startups in India and North America that typically offer ingenious solutions. Our mission is to transform them into rapid-growth businesses by providing in-depth support in the areas of business, marketing, financial and technical advice.

What are the advantages of developing tech startups in India?

M.L. Tandon: Entrepreneurship is coming of age right now in India. The passion for innovation makes the country an ideal environment for tech startups. That's why we're so passionate about helping startup companies grow.

Tandon Group has origins in India, United States and Singapore and while we have a deep understanding of all of these markets, we focus our efforts in India in particular because the country has a thriving economy. Indian entrepreneurs are passionate about solving big problems and making significant change.

We are proud of the role that Tandon Group has played in building a thriving electronic manufacturing industry in India. In the 1970s, the Indian electronic market was isolated and was not participating in the international market, due to severe import restrictions on electronic computers. We worked with the Indian government to simplify the operations for effective functioning and ease of doing business. We succeeded in creating tax free zones throughout India, resulting in increased production, foreign investment, increased exports and integrating the Indian electronic industry with international market and rapid economic growth ever since.

What do you feel are the biggest myths out there when it comes to developing tech startups in India?

M.L. Tandon: The global community does not recognize the level of innovation growing in India today. The entrepreneurial environment here is very dynamic, not just in terms of manufacturing components, but in new companies and ideas that are transforming industry.

What are some common misconceptions around the manufacturing and technology industry in India Industry?

M.L. Tandon: When I started the Tandon Mumbai plant in 1978, training the workforce was my top priority because I saw first-hand how corporate efficiency and flawless quality put IBM at the top of the global market. That's what I wanted for Tandon, but in India we have something called "Chalta hai" – meaning "It's good enough" or "The little things don't matter." But I knew that the little things do matter. Whenever I was on the production floor I would tell the workers "Chalta hai, nehi" or "Chalta hai is not okay!" Today, that spirit has spread to make our workforce second to none in the world. The misconception is in not realizing the tremendous progress in Indian manufacturing in recent years.

What are some of the little-known pitfalls or common mistakes founders make on the road to developing tech startups in India?

M.L. Tandon: The most important element for a successful business is having both technological and social innovation at the core of the business. However, when you are seeking to make change there will always be obstacles. They may involve recruiting the best talent, finding adequate funding, marketing efficiently, or training your workforce. That is true anywhere in the world, not just in India.

How can these pitfalls be avoided?

M.L. Tandon: Have the courage to step out of a system that no longer serves you or the world and do things in a different way. In the 1970s, dedicated labor in India was hard to find. The men who typically filled entry-level assembly positions would hop from town to town in search of other options. The costs of constantly training new workers added up quickly. So, I stopped hiring men. They could find jobs anywhere. Women, on the other hand, were legally prohibited from working at night. Families often didn't want them to work because of cultural reasons and no jobs were available to them anyway. But I saw these women as an untapped pool of industrial talent so I hired an all-female electronic assembly team. These women delivered a strong work ethic, loyalty and superior manual dexterity for high-precision electronics assembly.

In this case, the pitfall was the lack of a reliable labor pool, and the solution was to find a way to hire women. The goal isn't always to avoid pitfalls, but to use innovative thinking and a genuine willingness to embrace change so you can find solutions to inevitable challenges.

Can you share an example of how Tandon Group has helped a tech startup overcome these obstacles and succeed in India?

M.L. Tandon: Under the leadership of my sons, Sandeep, Jaideep and Sudeep, Tandon Group has focused on investing in tech startups and operating successful companies in India since the early 2000s. One of our most successful startup companies is FreeCharge, which was sold to SnapDeal in India's largest M&A internet deal. Sandeep co-founded FreeCharge with Kunal Shah, who was one of our business process managers at the time, and Sudeep joined the company later to scale it. Together, they helped FreeCharge get its operations off the ground and double its user base by tapping into the increased penetration of smartphones in India. This has enabled the market to leap from a 90-percent cash-based economy to cardless digital payments. Banks and telecommunication companies had struggled to get Indian consumers online. FreeCharge saw, and capitalized on, the opportunity to target a population with more access to mobile phones than access to the Internet. Getting consumers online required a major change in thinking, but FreeCharge had the courage to bring a good idea to market and they have transformed the way Indians pay.

To help FreeCharge find success despite the obstacles inherent in establishing an entirely new method of payment, Tandon Group helped in recruiting retail partners, nurturing relationships with banks and telecommunications companies to build out the payment platform, raising funds, driving sales, and facilitating hiring for key positions in the company. Each of those elements was necessary to overcoming the central obstacle.

Tandon Group has a rich history of innovation with a strong influence over the first floppy drives and first generation of IBM personal computers. What inspired you to start Tandon Group and continue to evolve into the startup incubator it is today?

M.L. Tandon: I remember the day I left India to pursue my master's degree in engineering at Purdue. As I climbed the steps to the airplane, my father pulled me aside and said, "Don't do anything that would give you, me or your country a bad name. The rest of you is free." It was a liberating moment for me because I knew I had my father's blessing to think and do differently, as long as I did something for the higher good. This continues to be a guiding principal and driver behind what Tandon Group continues to do today.

In some ways, the evolution to Tandon Group has been a natural one. I began my career at the IBM Development Lab in San Jose as an engineering manager. I returned home in 1967 to take on a key role at IBM India for nine years until IBM was asked to leave because of non-compliance with Indian Equity norms. When IBM was forced to close its plant in India in 1977, I, along with other key ex-IBMers, proposed to take over the plant. IBM accepted the proposal to give us all assets at the cost of 10 cents to a dollar as long as we employed everyone who had been working in the factory. As a result, we created a company called Pentax Engineering to provide products for the local market in India.

I started Tandon Magnetics in 1978 to supply recording heads to Tandon Corporation, which was founded by my brother Sirang Lal Tandon. We manufactured and exported magnetic heads and storage products as IBM's preferred supplier for floppy disk drives. We followed up the success of Tandon Magnetics with Tandon Motors in the 1990s, which focused on the manufacturing of motion technologies. That put Tandon Group on the global tech stage as a major supplier and partner for multinational companies including IBM, Hitachi and Toshiba.

In the beginning, I focused on improving manufacturing in terms of process, labor, trade and talent. Today, my family is working tirelessly to take Tandon Group to the next level.

My son Sandeep leads Tandon Group as managing director, focusing on identifying talented entrepreneurs and startups for our group to invest in and incubate. He also serves as chairman of Infinx Healthcare, a software provider for patient access and revenue cycle management for healthcare providers in the United States, as well as Syrma Technology, which continues to provide the world-class electronics manufacturing services the Tandon brand has been built upon.

Jaideep serves as joint director for Tandon Group, Infinx and Syrma and is focused on growing Infinx and Syrma in the U.S. and Europe, as well as building our investment portfolio in the U.S.

Sudeep, also a director of Tandon Group, helped FreeCharge more than double its user base and transaction volume, and onboard more than 500,000 merchants. Now, he is leading innovation at Infinx, specifically focused on artificial intelligence and robotic process automation for its patient access and accounts receivable software.

My daughters-in-law, Gauri and Radhika Tandon, launched a popular Indian-inspired fashion jewelry brand called Isharya after noticing a void in the global market for high quality and well-priced statement jewelry. The brand is carried online at Isharya.com, in international stores like Harvey Nichols, and at its own branded retail stores in Mumbai and New Delhi. Radhika also serves as CMO for Tandon Group, helping Infinx and Syrma with branding, marketing and sales enablement.

Sandeep, Jaideep, Sudeep, Gauri and Radhika carry on our rich history of solving industry problems. This is the common thread that has allowed our companies to change how people in India do business in the country and around the world, pioneer progressive workplaces in a state-directed economy and create technology that drives global change. It's why progress, entrepreneurship, innovation and excellence are part of our mission, and why we're committed to advancing technological and social innovation by helping next-generation startups in India succeed.

Can you share a lesson you learned early on, that still impacts how you do business today?

M.L. Tandon: Social innovation isn't just the right thing to do, it's a key marker of success. You are not only the creators of new standards and technologies; you are the creators of new perceptions that change people's lives for the better.

Also, you need to respect every individual on your team. No matter who they are, trust in their ability to do what you want them to do. No matter how big or small the job is, every person is important. Empower your team to take ownership of their work and keep your mind, ears and door open to them. Make your ideas big and keep your business small and nimble enough to succeed. Approach problems with innovation and tenacity, economically and socially. Think different and do well.

What's the most important question startup founders should ask themselves as they consider developing tech startups in India?

M.L. Tandon: India has a thriving economy and entrepreneurship is coming of age right now. Indian entrepreneurs are passionate about solving big problems and making significant change. It is an appealing place to launch your start up. But, you would be wise to consider how much you know about the culture, government and regulations. India is now more welcoming to tech startups than ever before, but you may need to find partners to help you navigate government rules and regulations.

How can startup founders find out more about Tandon Group and how you can help them?

M.L. Tandon: Tandon Group has offices in San Jose, Mumbai and Singapore. You can learn more at TandonGroup.com.

About M.L. Tandon

As Chairman of Tandon Group, M.L. Tandon is one of India's most distinguished pioneers and business leaders in the electronics manufacturing industry. He experienced the classic voyage and return story: From traveling to America to study and work – landing a managerial post at IBM in San Jose – to returning to India and launching several successful computer hardware and electronics manufacturing facilities in Mumbai.

During the late 1970s and 1980s, he led disk drive manufacturing operations for Tandon Corporation (later incorporated as Tandon Magnetics Corporation) in India, producing what became the industry standard double-sided floppy drive disk read-and-write heads.

Over the last 50 years, M.L. has contributed significantly to the electronic exports that gave rise to India's economy, helped advance the rights and family status of Indian women, and improved the lives of individuals worldwide through technological innovation. He is actively involved in improving trade and promoting exports from India, spearheading several associations, councils and committees.

Today, Tandon Group is a technology catalyst that owns several successful businesses and provides resources to next-generation startups in India and North America. Tandon Group's mission is to transform them into rapid-growth businesses by providing in-depth support in the areas of business, marketing, financial and technical advice.

BUSINESS NAME
Tandon Group

WEBSITE
TandonGroup.com

EMAIL
info@tandongroup.com

LOCATION
San Jose, Mumbai, Singapore

FACEBOOK
Facebook.com/TandonGroup.in

TWITTER
Twitter.com/TandonGroup

LINKEDIN
LinkedIn.com/in/Manohar-lal-m-l-Tandon-ab1808b7/

How to Move Forward
After Bankruptcy

Bankruptcy is frightening. Many people wonder, "What will bankruptcy do to my credit score? What will my friends say? What will my family say?" People seeking help are asking difficult questions and making difficult choices. "Do I pay my mortgage this month, or do I pay my high interest credit card? Do I pay rent this month, or do I pay my car note? Where can I turn for help?"

While there are legal issues associated with bankruptcy, most questions and concerns remain more practical than anything else, and oftentimes just as important. Debt brings about anxiety, stress, shame and embarrassment. People believe they have let themselves and their families down. They feel that they have nowhere to turn.

Matthew J. Cherney of Cherney Law Firm, LLC and his team are experts at helping their clients wade through the problems that make up consumer bankruptcy. They will help you reduce your stress and help get you back on the road to financial stability.

Conversation with Matthew J. Cherney

Matt, tell us a little bit more about yourself and your law firm. Obviously, bankruptcy is a big issue. Is bankruptcy all that you deal with?

Matthew J. Cherney: I've been practicing exclusively in bankruptcy and debt related matters for about 13 years. I started practicing in my hometown of Chicago, Illinois back in 2005 and practiced there at a large bankruptcy firm for approximately four years.

And the firm I was with provided me an opportunity to move down here to Georgia. They were expanding their practice into other markets and I was afforded the opportunity to move down here with my wife and act as managing attorney at the firm down here in Georgia.

I stayed with them for about another five years and then started my own practice. I've been in private practice for myself, dealing exclusively in debt related matters, for about six years now and focus primarily on consumer bankruptcy cases, specifically chapter 7 and chapter 13.

What are some of the issues that people are having these days with debt relief and what kind of solutions are there available for them?

Matthew J. Cherney: In all my years of practice I've run the gambit and run into almost every sort of circumstance that you can imagine. I've been doing this quite a long time now.

I have clients anywhere from people who are unemployed to where they just can't begin to service any portion of their debt. I have clients who are underemployed. These are clients who made good money and at the time, they were able to service what would have otherwise been a manageable amount of debt relative to their income, but now their current income simply doesn't allow them to maintain their payments on their debt while still maintaining a certain standard of living.

I have clients who fell ill, recently hospitalized, who can't afford to maintain or begin to pay what is an astronomical amount of debt for their medical bills. I have clients with tax debts, I have clients who for a host of different reasons simply fell behind on house payments, vehicle payments, and perhaps it's not necessarily a matter of maintaining these payments going forward but for unforeseen circumstances, they just simply cannot catch their payments up.

One thing that I found over the years that dealing with debt brings with it potential legal issues but it's not always just legal problems for individuals. I found that the larger issues are emotional.

Many of my clients deal with anxiety, stress, shame, embarrassment, and all things associated with the underlying debt and they feel like they maybe let themselves down. Perhaps they feel like they've let their families down. They feel like they've got nowhere to turn.

A lot of this stems from debt and having creditors that might be harassing you or trying to collect from you and I found that a lot of the collateral issues are largely emotional. That's something that's not lost on me which is why I really try to be an advocate for clients and try to show them that I understand that these things are larger than just the debt itself.

What is the most common reason people get into debt?

Matthew J. Cherney: It changes over the years. In good economic times, I found that it comes from unforeseen expenses, household expenses, illness. During less than stellar economic times, it may come from unemployment, underemployment and just inability to service the current debt that they have. There are times where you make a good living, you provide for your family, you're able to afford the monthly payments associated with your debt and then there comes a time where you're just not able to do it anymore and people are faced with the idea of, "Do I provide for my family? Do I pay my mortgage payment, my lease payment on my apartment? Do I pay my car loan? What do I do? Where do I turn?" These are the harsh realities and circumstances that face a lot of my clients.

We have been recovering from the recession back in 2007, 2008 when the market crashed but it's been pretty good for the last 10 years. Do you see things in the market suggesting that it's going to turn again?

Matthew J. Cherney: Well, the signs before were very tied to the housing market and that was one thing that most people point to when they talk about the recession and it affected a lot of people back, around the time that I started to practice in 2006 to 2008. A lot of people point to the housing market.

But now the signs aren't necessarily tied to that. What I'm seeing are things tied to lending, just lending in general, specifically vehicles. That's one big thing, subprime vehicle loans. I see a bubble really getting ready to burst there.

Traditionally, vehicle loans were a four or five-year loan. Now you're seeing some vehicle loans stretched out as far as seven or eight years and often, these sorts of subprime loans are going to carry with them rather high interest rates, 18, 25 percent.

Some people, unfortunately, might not be as savvy to look at the amount of interest that they pay on a vehicle over eight years. Sometimes people are paying 60% more than what the vehicle may even be worth.

Student loans are another huge area where something at some point is going to have to give. I don't know if that's going to be by the intervention of Congress but that is something that is certainly coming to a head. There is so much student loan debt and folks, no matter what their financial circumstances are in life, are having difficulty in dealing with these payments. That's not just someone who is working for minimum wage. These are professionals, doctors, lawyers.

These sorts of student loan payments are just becoming very unmanageable. So, the signs of a recession are becoming more and more apparent, not necessarily tied to housing but more towards things like vehicle loans, student loans, etc.

When somebody does get into trouble, what kind of options are available for them?

Matthew J. Cherney: I meet with clients all the time, potential clients or just individuals who might be looking for some sort of solution to deal with their debt. That could be the possibility of trying to negotiate lower payments or negotiate settlements on a particular debt.

Bankruptcy, while an option, isn't always someone's first option. A lot of times the first thing a potential client and I speak about is the fact that no one wants to find themselves here in my office and having the conversations that we ultimately have. A lot of people might feel embarrassed or they're already dealing with anxiety and stress and perhaps shame.

We sit and we have an open conversation about what options might be available to them and if they're not in a financial position to negotiate any sort of payment or settlement, we can always look at bankruptcy options, be that a chapter 7 or chapter 13. That is some sort of reorganization mandated by the court that allows individuals to either eliminate their debt in full or perhaps reorganize their debt, which is putting together a plan that allows an individual to pay back their debt or a portion thereof in a more economically viable way that suits their budget. Something that's not just based upon the debt itself but based on their ability to pay.

Break down chapter 7 and the chapter 13 bankruptcy because I know a lot of people just need clarification on why you would use either one.

Matthew J. Cherney: Chapter 7 is going to be designed for individuals who do not have the financial means to pay back their debt. That's referred to as the complete bankruptcy. If someone's doing their own research on bankruptcy or learning a little bit about bankruptcy, the first thing that they see is the idea of chapter 7.

Chapter 7 is there to deal with things like unsecured debt. Unsecured debt could be credit cards, medical bills or personal unsecured loans where they haven't pledged anything as collateral for the loan. What we're illustrating in chapter 7 is that one cannot reasonably pay back their debt within a period of time however nominal that payment will be.

Chapter 13 is designed for individuals who may not qualify for chapter 7. That could be either based upon that fact they filled a chapter 7 within the last eight years or perhaps they make too much money to do a chapter 7 because there are income criteria for chapter 7. Chapter 13 is designed for those individuals who may be trying to protect an asset like a vehicle that they may have fallen behind on that's in danger of being repossessed or to prevent home foreclosure. They may have fallen behind on their mortgage payments and chapter 13 allows them to consolidate all of their debt and propose to pay it back to their creditors in some form over a period of anywhere from three to five years.

What does this do to the credit? Is that a big fear that holds people back?

Matthew J. Cherney: Certainly, one's credit score is of concern and a lot of times when we sit and we discuss what option's going to suit the individual best, one thing they ask is, "Well, what's it going to do to my credit?"

My response to that, while not dodging the question, is often times, "What does your credit look like right now?" If I'm meeting with someone, chances are their credit might not necessarily be in the best state of repair.

If the credit is not necessarily in the best state of repair currently, then the less effect the bankruptcy is going to have on that individual's credit.

Now, I do have folks who are trying to simply be preemptive. They say, "I've been making my minimum payments on my car. I've never missed a payment. I've never missed a payment to anybody but for reasons x, y, and z, I see that at some point, that's no longer going to be the case."

Those individuals often have pretty good credit scores. The only thing that might be affecting their credit score is their debt to income ratio. They're paying out a lot of debt, maybe just barely and relative to their income which could be affecting their credit score, but otherwise, they've maintained payments all along. The effect on those folks' credit is going to be a little bit larger because we'll presume that their credit score is higher. The higher your credit score, the more effect the bankruptcy is going to have on it but, I really try to convey to folks, especially those who really need the relief is we've got to shift our thinking here and shift our focus from what is the effect going to be on my credit to how do I start over? How do I get into a better financial situation? How do I change my focus and shift it from, what's my credit score going to be...to how do I get out of this debt?

If we can shift the focus to that, people say, "Well, okay. I can put the thoughts about what the effect's going to be on the back burner and just look forward rather than look behind."

Other than the credit issue, what are some other fears clients have?

Matthew J. Cherney: A lot of it has to do with rehabilitating. Where am I going to be a month after bankruptcy? A year after bankruptcy? What is my credit going to look like and what are ways that I can rehabilitate my credit?

Those are certainly concerns but might be better explained as misconceptions. A lot of times, people feel that well, if I file bankruptcy, I'm going to lose everything that I have. I'm going to lose my car, I'm going to lose my house. Frankly, that's more the exception than it is the rule. People in the immediate sense worry about what bankruptcy is going to do to their current circumstance, but they are also concerned about rehabilitation and where they'll find themselves after bankruptcy is over.

How do you save those kind of assets like the cars and the homes?

Matthew J. Cherney: Well, if someone is delinquent on their vehicle payment or if they are delinquent on their home mortgage, we accomplish that through chapter 13. In a chapter 13, the client needs to meet the requirements, which ultimately is that they have regular income.

Regular income could be classified in many different ways. It's not just having W2 wages. It could be self-employment, it could be fixed income, social security, child support income, rental income if they rent out a room in their house or if they have property that they lease to another individual. Regular income is the criteria.

What we're able to do specifically with those debts where the individual has a delinquent vehicle or house note, we're able to take those debts and pay them back through a chapter 13. Vehicles specifically would be paid in full, subject to certain modifications perhaps to the interest rate but generally, the vehicle would be paid in full through the chapter 13 plan.

With house notes, the plan is to be able to take those mortgage arrears, the amount that the individual's currently behind at the time of filling and propose to pay those arrears back through the chapter 13 plan. Certain districts in the US are different as to how the mortgage lender is paid going forward.

Here in the northern district of Georgia where I practice, the plans are structured in such a way to where the plan only contemplates paying back the arrears. The individual is then obligated to make those mortgage payments going forward with the next consecutive month.

For example, if an individual filed chapter 13 on the third of the month, the chapter 13 plan would cover paying back all mortgage arrears through December. The individual would then be responsible to maintain and resume making mortgage payments in January.

By having a plan that contemplates paying back those debts, it prevents a vehicle creditor from repossessing the vehicle. It also prevents a mortgage lender from foreclosing on the property.

What are some of the warnings signs of bankruptcy?

Matthew J. Cherney: It comes in many different ways. As I said earlier, it's not always just going to be about missing a payment or having a creditor that is calling or sending letters. A lot has to do with the emotional side of it too.

If someone is getting anxious about a particular bill they have coming up and whether or not they should make their payment to a particular creditor on a credit card or if I do that, how am I going to pay my light bill or pay my gas bill? Those are warning signs. Or, if you're using your credit cards to pay your normal household expenses and juggling balances between one card to the next. Or, stressing about having the ability to meet your financial obligations when that time of the month comes. I think those would qualify as some warning signs.

Do you feel right now that most people are living above their means?

Matthew J. Cherney: That is always going to be relative to their financial circumstances. What I'm seeing currently is that incomes are starting to rebound. People are starting to recover just purely from employment. People are going from being unemployed to being employed so, that doesn't always mean that your current employment situation is sufficient enough to maintain your debt and make those payments each month. Your income before might have been considerably more. Your income now might be less than it was and you just can't afford to do it. I don't necessarily see that people are living above their means as much as they're really scratching and crawling to be able to make their payments as they are now.

Give me some examples of people that you have dealt with. What kind of position were they in? How were you able to help them and ultimately, what was the outcome for their lives?

Matthew J. Cherney: As I said earlier, I have clients that run the gambit from unemployment, underemployment, medical related issues, tax-related issues, mortgage, and vehicle-related issues. One thing I try to convey to all of my clients or people that I meet with is that ultimately, bankruptcy can be an option.

Nearly every individual that I meet with shares these same feelings. After I meet with them, they begin to realize that there are options. Most even start to feel a bit of relief after the first consultation. I find that it's simply perhaps just having someone to talk to, just an objective person to speak with, someone with the experience who can tell them that they understand their situation. They don't have to feel like they're being judged.

I can't count the number of times that clients have told me that they'd wish they'd at least come to speak with me sooner, especially after the process is over. Again, whether that's completely eliminating their debt, not having to worry about how they're going to make a certain payment on a particular month and they can then reapportion that money to other areas of their life, providing for their family.

They wish they had taken the step sooner and ultimately, every client that I have helped ultimately winds up happy that they met with me and that they went through the process.

If somebody has some of those issues that we've been talking about today and they want to get in contact with you, what is the best way for them to do that?

Matthew J. Cherney: They can reach me via phone. I've got a great assistant here that works with me. Her name is Denise and can be reached via phone at **770-485-4141**. That's my main office number. **770-485-4141**.

Often people are a little bit hesitant to want to speak to someone on the phone so they can always go to my website which is cherneylaw.com or contact me via email at mcherney@cherneylawfirm.com.

At my website, you can also set up appointments via text. You can text and nine times out of ten I'm going to be the individual that is responding to the text messages. That is certainly something that I've learned over the years, that I try to bring to my practice, which is more of a personal touch.

So, if people call in and you need to speak with me and you want to speak with me, you can speak with me. If you want to text, you can text and I welcome that opportunity.

About Matthew J. Cherney

Attorney Matthew Cherney, founder of Cherney Law Firm LLC received his Bachelor's Degree from Carthage College in Kenosha, Wisconsin before going on to receive his Juris Doctorate from Western Michigan University (The Thomas M. Cooley Law School) in Lansing, Michigan.

After graduating law school, Matthew was admitted to the State Bar of Illinois and began his legal career in his hometown of Chicago, Illinois, where he represented clients in all areas of debt relief for a large bankruptcy firm. In 2008, he moved to Georgia and was admitted to the State Bar of Georgia. Over the years, he gained experience at both large-volume and mid-volume consumer bankruptcy firms before starting his own practice in 2012.

Mr. Cherney now seeks to provide personal attention and counseling for all his clients, working personally with them from their initial consultation all the way through the completion of their case. Having represented thousands of clients since he began practicing law, Matthew has helped to improve many individuals' quality of life and to decrease their financial stress.

At Cherney Law Firm LLC, clients can expect the highest quality legal representation alongside thoughtful counseling and attention to detail. Mr. Cherney dedicates his time to properly investigating every possible avenue of debt relief for his clients before simply stepping into bankruptcy. Seeking to make each consumer that comes to him for legal aid as comfortable as possible, he keeps his clients in the loop with every step he takes.

Attorney Matthew Cherney is licensed to practice in all state courts of both Georgia and Illinois, as well as in the federal courts for the Northern and Middle Districts of Georgia, and in the Northern District of Illinois. Matthew is also married and enjoys spending time with his wife and his son.

WEBSITE
CherneyLaw.com

PHONE
770-485-4141

EMAIL

contact@cherneylaw.com

ADDRESS

Marietta Office:

1744 Roswell Road Marietta, GA 30062

Woodstock Office:

103 Springfield Drive, Suite 204 Woodstock, GA 30188

Digital Marketing – Kung Fu Style

Dr. Joe Schaefer is a master strategist in the realm of digital marketing. He guides owners and teams to build well-oiled sales or lead generation machines. He has a unique background. Dr. Joe is an actual published neuroscience researcher with a PhD from the University of Texas. He is also Master Joe, a seventh-degree black built in Shaolin Kung Fu and he started and oversees 10 full-time schools.

In his agency, Dr. Joe has personally worked with over 500 business owners in the digital marketing realm since 2002 and he brings marketing, science, and coaching together into a step by step process to help business owners create that well-oiled leads, or sales generating machine and master the discipline of marketing to build solid, profitable businesses.

Conversation with Dr. Joe Schaefer

Tell us a little bit more about who it is that you help. I know you have a varied and studied past, but what kind of companies do you help with digital marketing?

Dr. Schaefer: In the digital marketing world, I began serving clients in 2002. Then in 2008 my partner and I were one of only a handful of companies in the world to build and run our own custom software as a service (SAAS) engine to deliver borderless frameless videos over websites. In the years following I helped hundreds of clients by discovering what made their business different. I had to write a 30 to 60 second script that distilled that story and the best call to action in their website so they could realize better leads or sales. This entire plan had to work or we promised to re-shoot the video again and again until they got results. This was like compressing a lifetime of consulting into just a few years. Each client wanted the best results and consultative approach to uncovering their story. I had to quickly learn to get to the heart of their marketing message, Unique Selling Proposition (USP) and best call to action and conversion method.

Now we work with every kind of business ranging from owner operator and small businesses, up to companies with 50 or 60 locations. For seven years, I ran the digital marketing campaigns for about 200 auto dealerships, gathering over one hundred thousand leads a year for them. My preferred client now is an owner operator or marketing decision maker since it allows us to test and adapt at greater speeds and leverage the true power of the internet.

I understand you are also a 7th degree black belt in martial arts and even have a PhD in Neuroscience from the University of Texas. How do these very different backgrounds help you to serve your clients?

Dr. Schaefer: Well first and foremost I enjoy teaching and bringing clarity to complex topics, that is what brings me the most joy. Once I understand something I feel an absolute need to share that understanding with someone else. I also feel compelled to inspire and help people transform at a personal level. Bringing your own business into being is a deeply personal pursuit and business owners are completely overwhelmed by the digital marketing revolution. They are often like lambs lead to the slaughter and sold every possible platform and program until they are bled dry. My science background provided opportunities to teach, as well as learning to use research and data to evolve new strategies and strengthen the findings.

I can see how Neuroscience is useful within the realm of research and development of websites and marketing strategies, but can you talk more about how martial arts can be connected to business growth?

Dr. Schaefer: Martial arts were developed over fifteen hundred years ago and were considered one of the foundational disciplines for every scholar and leader in ancient China. These days martial arts are mostly for personal transformation, health or sport, no longer for life and death situations. The techniques and training paradigms are still meant to produce lethality but thankfully we don't need that part. In business, it is really a life or death struggle to survive and just like martial arts, there is a progression of milestones and development between the launch of any new business and eventual operation maturity.

I have found that my 3 decades of teaching Kung Fu has created a unique operating system in me. I think in terms of milestone driven development and growth. I see my role as equal parts, marketing strategist, troubleshooter, educator and coach.

Do you have a standardized regimen for your business clients or is each a different process?

Dr. Schaefer: Each time an owner or marketing team comes to see me, they are in a different state of confusion, dysfunction or chaos. Each stakeholder has their own pet digital platform or tactic that they want to use. This bias could come from their own daily experience or a colleague that used that tactic successfully. We start each engagement with a discovery process to first find out what their long-term goals are and what assets that they might be under-leveraging in their business We ask questions like, "What industry is this? Where's your audience going to be? Will they be searching for your product on Google? Are you going to reach your audience on Facebook? Are you going to reach them with Banner Ads, or Search Ads? Do you need SEO?" Or is this a product that is new enough that no one is searching for it. Why would you invest in SEO if no one's going to be searching for you? It may not be the best method.

What would you say are two or three of the most common problems that you end up focusing on?

Dr. Schaefer: There is an intense focus on technology and platforms in digital marketing. Many of these platforms are actually very complicated engines that are powerful in the right hands. However, they are being sold as a DIY platform that puts the power in the business owner's hands. Remember it also puts the responsibility for failure squarely in their hands. Remember that during the gold rush, the people who made the most money were not the prospectors, but were the people selling the wheelbarrow's and the shovels, and the pickaxes.

The most powerful and famous of these platforms is the Google Ads system. That platform is littered with the broken-hearted business owners that lost their money and their faith in digital marketing after a failed attempt to place and manage their own ad campaigns.

All companies are starting at different steps in their marketing, but they can become quite fixated on specific tactics in digital marketing. But very often, that may not even be the correct tactic for their industry or for where they currently are in their marketing development. Identifying where they are at identifies the next step in their process, or the first step, so that's the most challenging part. For example, people have heard of SEO, or they heard of social media, and that becomes the focus of their campaign, even though they might not have an adequate conversion process in their website. A way to turn visitors into leads or sales.

The third problem is actually the most difficult to beat. If people didn't have this problem they could defeat all the others. It is the perspective of where they are in their own stage of marketing development and the staying power that comes with that understanding.

It seems like business owners have the shiny object syndrome where they're jumping from one thing to the next without the discipline, and discipline is so important in martial arts, but even more so in business, when within the first five years, I think the stats are 80% of businesses fail.

Dr. Schaefer: Yes, let's take a lesson here from martial art training. It may take you 10 years to reach your goal in martial arts and what I find with many business owners is six months into a new venture, if they haven't reached their dream level, they start to lose their edge and believe that their idea won't work. If they were in my Kung Fu class, I would say to them, "Hey, you're only like a blue belt right now, so calm down, you're right where you're supposed to be. The vision you have of your business is about 3rd degree black belt level of achievement and that typically takes a lot more training and education. So where are you on your progressive journey? Right where you should be based on your level so far of training.

With this kind of long term perspective, they are able to weather the ups and downs inherent to any journey or transformation. Bringing a business into the world is an act of sheer mind over matter and requires no less than being a martial art master.

How do you balance that aspect of business, which is, I've got to be in business, I've got to make money to cover all my bills and to pay for my standard of living, to "Well, you're still a blue belt, yet you haven't quite made it to the level that you want. How do you have that conversation?

Dr. Schaefer: To quote the famous Jim Rohn, "Don't bring your need to the marketplace, bring your skill". If you joined my school and said, "I have never trained, but I have a death match in six months and I have to get ready," Then my answer would be you are going to have to train 8 hours a day and pay me a bunch of money to stand there and take you through it. It is no different with business. If you wanted to take your business from white to black belt that fast, then you will have to spend vast amounts of time and money to overcome the time-dependent nature of growth.

You seemed to favor the strategic long term view of marketing can you explain the difference between a tactic and the strategy behind a digital marketing campaign.

Dr. Schaefer: That is a pretty big subject. The father of modern advertising, Claude Hopkins named his most famous book "Scientific Advertising". Written in 1923, that book told us that the only strategy that works is testing and adapting our message and media based on data and results. He would have loved the internet which is the ultimate playground for this. I 100% agree with his notion that we can never know what will work in our marketing, we can only test and refine. Our clients are the only experts on what message will reach them. So, in other words there are no tactics I always recommend, and then strategy is always ready – fire – aim.

After hundreds of clients there must be some recurring challenges. Do you have any general digital marketing advice you can give without knowing specifics?

Dr. Schaefer: Well, most owners are too focused on getting more traffic. There's really a 50/50 problem, traffic and conversion, right? You can have plenty of traffic to your site and you don't convert that traffic, then you're still in trouble, and if you have great conversion, no traffic, you still have the problem, but what I find is the typical owners or marketing teams, they focus on the traffic end of things without focusing on the conversion.

That is just like pouring an endless amount of water into a leaky bucket. It doesn't matter how much water you pour in; you cannot fill the bucket. What we do is we work on the bucket first. Seal up the website, create clear paths to conversion, multiple paths, try to appeal to the four persona types that come to the website and make sure that all the marketing dollars spent after we do that are spent bringing people into the site.

I think that is an extremely important point. If people are listening in, they've got to realize that the conversion part of your website and what it's saying, is more important than getting the traffic, because again, money can buy you traffic, but it's not going to buy you that conversion. Now, you have a doctorate in Neuroscience and you know how the mind works, so what kind of things on a website are going to get the mind in the right state to buy? Or along that progressive journey to buy?

Dr. Schaefer: All the research shows that decisions about whether to bounce from a site are actually made in less than a second. We always talk about you've got six seconds and there's all these kinds of anecdotal amounts of time out there, but actually they can show the decision to bounce is made in milliseconds, not seconds. They may stay there for a little bit longer, but they're actually destined to leave the site.

Imagine you are in a shopping mall and there are 10 identical shoe stores standing side by side. That is like the first page of Google search results except there are actually 20+ results side by side. This creates an extreme "Attention Deficit" style of browsing that we all see online. Being a scientist I need to create my own jargon so I coined a term called "Back Pressure". It describes the mental state of someone faced with an overwhelming number of choices on Google. There is more pressure pushing them out of your site than keeping them in the site. There is more promise of clarity back on the Google search result page than in any one particular website. You have to fight tooth and nail to keep someone in your site against 19 other identical store fronts and back pressure.

There's arguments out there, on both sides of the fence here, and I'm not sure which one I belong to myself. There's the SEO aspect that says you got to have all these words on the page and the content in order it to be found, and then you've got the other side, which is what you were talking about, people making decisions in less than a second. They don't even have time to read text.

What has to be on the website in order for them just to stay around to read what's on it?

Dr. Schaefer: There are four or five key features that they can immediately scan and skim on that website. Some of the most important ones of course, they have to see some kind of visual representation, either text and/or pictures that match what their need is. Obviously, they're searching for some item or some product. They need to see it when they land there. There needs to be some credibility, and this is of course your world Neil, authority and credibility factors that tell them unconsciously within milliseconds that this is a reputable vendor or provider of that service. There needs to be some kind of a call to action, some kind of a path that they immediately see what their job is in the website.

That's what I call trust triggers. You're looking for things that indicate trust right away. Lots of emblems from the industry awards or things like that are going to catch the attention. Just to have people stick around for a little bit longer.

What are some of the misconceptions for you as a digital marketer that you hear from your clients?

Dr. Schaefer: They think that there's some kind of a new tactic that everybody's using that will save them. They are looking for some web 2.0 or 3.0 trick that's going to subvert reality for them. It's going to help them beat others in some kind of tricky way. That's what I think is the greatest misconception.

When what is actually missing is some good old fashioned thinking, creative thinking about the website and the unbiased ability to step into the mental shoes of your website visitor. You asked whether conversion might be the missing component but that fix starts with creative thinking. You spend $100.00 to bring 100 visitors to your website, and you only convert let's say three of them to a lead. If you want six leads instead of three, now you have to spend $200.00 to double your leads. However, if you can double your conversion rate, then all you have to do is spend $100.00 to get double the leads. That math can change your world dramatically if you have multiple sources of traffic coming into your site. All of the sources perform better when you have a higher conversion rate.

That's right, and not all traffic comes from the internet either.

Dr. Schaefer: That's exactly correct.

Some traffic is word of mouth and networking events or whatever it might be, they're definitely going to find out more about you once they hear something about you.

Dr. Schaefer: I agree, and some of the biggest winners, some of my clients who have capitalized the most on this are ones that use a large amount of traditional media still. TV, radio, newspaper, they use digital and they use traditional, and when we win in the website, we win big, because they're putting the real-world money into multiple ways of getting traffic to the site.

When the prospect lands on the site, they generally have a need or a problem that they need to get solved. How do you talk to that specifically on these websites?

Dr. Schaefer: Yes. They have a need and I refer to it as two ways. There's a long-term need and there's a today need. The long-term need is if I'm looking for a financial advisor, then my long-term need is I want to build a retirement. I want someone to manage my retirement funds for me. The today need is often completely different from the long-term need. The "today need" is almost always informational in nature. Very often it is about pricing or the details of the service.

I read a story recently about Jeff Bezos and the way he thinks about his business and he's thinking 20 years in advance. He's not thinking about tomorrow all the time, which I think is definitely the recipe for success, so getting that strategy in place and being able to build gradually on it like the belts that you talk about in martial arts is the way to success.

Dr. Schaefer: That's a perfect set up Neil for me. Talking about martial arts, when you're training in something like that, like the martial arts, it is a long-term decade, or decade's long journey, but you have to make daily decisions, and you have to plan that work. If you don't do something daily or weekly, you're not going to reach those goals. It's a daily battle, but the success is years away, so you have to have your sight on the future.

Dr. Joe, we've definitely covered a lot today, a lot of great information. If there's something that we didn't touch on that you'd like to mention before we go, what might that be?

Dr. Schaefer: I think this has been great. I really enjoyed combining these neuroscience, martial arts and digital marketing. I haven't told many of my clients they're even on this plan, but it's certainly the unwritten plan in my head for them. It's a very long plan, for instance, if you're on the 10-year plan, you think differently than if you're on the "I have to succeed in six months" plan. When someone comes to me and they're disappointed because they haven't achieved their goals yet and I find out they're only six months in, I want to say, "Hey, you're only a blue belt, where are you on your long-term mastery plan". If you keep at it for 10 years, I guarantee you will achieve whatever you're looking for, whether it's business success, whether it's personal development, whether you want to be a thought leader in some area, you will be there if you stick with it for 10 years, so that's really the thrust of all of my work.

That's so many people's problems, they just quit before they reach the top, but sticking with it and having that discipline is definitely a trait that more business people need. Well, Dr. Joe, this has been awesome. If people want to reach out to you and get more knowledge and advice from you or have you look at their business and the strategy that they have, what is the best way for them to do that?

Dr. Schaefer: Well, you can visit my website, motiliti.com or email me joe@motiliti.

It sounds like there is a book coming with these belt ideas. Is that something that you're working on?

Dr. Schaefer: Yes, because everybody is so familiar with the martial art world and belts, I decided to go ahead and lay this out so people can work from the end. Like Stephen Covey says, "Work with the end in mind," work backwards from your goal and create their own milestone belt plan for whatever it is they're trying to achieve. It works in business, but also any personal goal or desire.

Good luck getting that together.

Dr. Schaefer: Thank you.

About Dr. Joseph Schaefer

Dr. Joe Schaefer is the co-founder of Motiliti Inc, a marketing agency in Austin Texas. He has been serving clients since 2002 with search engine marketing, video marketing, message development and social media advertising.

Along with marketing, Dr. Joe is a published neuroscience researcher with a PhD from University of Texas. He was awarded Young Researcher of the Year In his field for the study of the neural basis of behaviors. He has a lifelong passion for Chinese martial arts and is currently a 7th degree black belt. In that world, he is known as Master Joe and has opened 9 schools. He combines the data-driven approach of science with a deep understanding of strategy that comes from 30+ years spent training and teaching Kung Fu. He has served over 500 business clients and taught Kung Fu to several thousand adults and kids.

Dr. Joe's marketing consulting approach is completely unique. He brings a completely distinctive set of skills to the table and is equal parts digital marketing expert, educator and inspiring coach. His clients come to rely on his ability to troubleshoot and solve problems by finding the un-leveraged assets and using novel and disruptive approaches.

WEBSITE
Motiliti.com

PHONE
(512) 387-6705

EMAIL
joe@motiliti.com

A Unique Business Philosophy Creates a Success Formula for Happy Clients and Happy Workers

"My life has been an exciting journey with a strong, tight family, quality upbringing, and of course the ups and downs like everyone else. 'What doesn't kill you will only make you stronger' is a motto I live by. And with every mistake made is an opportunity for betterment. I have learned to change my way of thinking about things that I have to do which I don't like into something that I love and can prosper from. I love sports and hobbies that require physical activity which makes all elements of health essential to me! I have played hockey for well over 40 years and get on the ice during the day five times a week and play on two leagues at night. I love slalom waterskiing, motorcycling, snowmobiling, and snowboarding. I travel to exotic places over the winter to recharge my battery and escape undesirable weather.

My business has been a constant change in size, operation, business style and types of clients and projects we accept. I like to keep it manageable so we all can enjoy our daily duties and projects. It is my perception that we should all be grateful for each other, and build each other up, so we can enjoy what we do, making us all more efficient and happy so we can take pride in what we've done. I believe we should only take on clients that make "sense" or are a "good fit" for us to survive properly. That way the company, workers, and clients are all happy in the end. That's a triple win in my book.

Conversation with Don Johanson

Tell us a little bit about your business and the types of clients you're helping.

Don Johanson: Typically, we deal with clients who are looking for an honest experience that fits the best project for their needs. Moreover, part of our business style is, not necessarily trying to sell particular projects or services, but to best inform the client what will and won't work, as far as their needs, the end result and what they're looking for.

So, you're really about listening to the client and finding out really what they need, versus just out there selling painting services.

Don Johanson: Exactly right. And sometimes some of the folks think that they need something, and typically that's because another contractor has told them that this is what they need. Sometimes that's not the right choice to fit with what they're genuinely looking for, or for longevity in the project, or whatever time constraint they may have, or whatever their needs may be. It's more about trying to find a way to solve the client's problem and create the exact type of project that will work for their needs.

I bet they really appreciate that. Moreover, they'll probably be back with more business and referrals because they like the honest approach, which unfortunately in this day and age isn't always that common.

Don Johanson: Yes, I find that being honest with folks creates a lot of confidence between our clients and us. And sometimes, we even wind up telling clients things they don't necessarily want to hear, but ultimately what's best for their needs. So, the connections we do make are extremely good connections, and typically our clients stay with us for a long time.

So, Don, what led you into the field and got you started doing this?

Don Johanson: Right out of high school, I went to college, and I started painting. What I really liked about it was there was always an end result. So, you'd start off with something, and at the end, you had an end result, and typically it was a client who was extremely happy with how the project turned out or how it had changed their environment whether it be their office or their home. Also, that end result made it feel like theirs; whether it was the color, the texture, the particular style, or whatever it may be, there was an end result. It always made me feel good coming home from work. And not only was I happy because I improved and made somebody happy, but the client was delighted as well. It's just like a person who goes to work at their job, and if their bosses are ecstatic with the work they've done, they feel great about themselves. That's what got me into the field.

You've been doing this for a long time. You just can't get that type of experience and know-how anywhere else. It's working in the field since you were in college, fine-tuning your skills and helping clients get these end results and feeling good about it. You bring a lot to the table.

Don Johanson: Thank you. It's true and that's a nice thing for me because I can understand the craftsman in the field and the clients as well because I've been in the field and I have that experience. There are many business owners nowadays in these small types of businesses, particularly the trades, who don't necessarily understand the problems that may arise out on the job site and then point fingers in the wrong directions which creates a bad attitude with workers or clients or both. Instead of doing it like that, we try and problem solve it. And because I have the experience of working in the field for so many years, I understand the many things that can happen on a job. I can change things quickly and, I'm able to rectify it, because I was there, and I've done that.

So, along the way, I talk to a lot of business owners and entrepreneurs, and there's always something or someone who inspires them along the way. Can you think of anyone or anything that encouraged you and helped you get to where you are today?

Don Johanson: My grandfather. He was actually in the trades years ago. When I was a kid, I used to go on jobs with him. It was always about working with my hands, and it was about being busy and a hands-on type of experience. I remember that as a kid; he was always happy when he put on the tools. He was an old-school guy, so when he was done, he'd put down the tools, and he'd go fishing and forget about it. He just seemed like a happy guy. I see a lot of folks, they go to work or they go to their jobs or their businesses, and it seems these environments run them into the ground. I saw that he was always a happy-go-lucky guy. I'm also a hands-on guy, and so that's what inspired me to get into the field.

It sounds like your grandfather really lived the motto "Life is meant to be lived!" He worked hard, he played hard, and he enjoyed every moment of it. It wasn't like many people today, who work for Friday because they can't stand what they're doing. He loved what he did and when he was done, he went out and lived life. Moreover, you've taken that same philosophy as well which is very inspiring.

Don Johanson: Right. The most significant part of our business which I really enjoy is we have really good people who work for us and we have really, really good clients who work with us. And it seems like there's never problems and, if there is any type of situation, it's just one resolution away from being rectified. So, there's never any finger-pointing. There's never any problems that go on and create any uncomfortable situations between our administrative staff and our workers or our clients.

Moreover, if a problem may arise, we have it handled almost immediately. So, it seems like everybody stays really happy. As a matter of fact, earlier today, I met with a couple of the guys who work for me. They said how they loved working for me and the reason why is because our clients were so nice and because the projects were clearly spelled out and they knew exactly what was needed and what they were going to be doing.

It's just a very smooth experience, not only for our clients but our workers too. The more we can keep everybody happy and enjoying what they do, the better the jobs are which the guy's complete. So yeah, I do like the fact that everybody seems to be happy and nobody finger points and nothing's really a problem. So, I do enjoy being in this business and hope to be for a long time, and hopefully, I can carry this business into a second generation where I can hand it off to my family.

I think I see a book title coming there, "Happy Leader, Happy Workers, Happy Clients," where you tell your story and unique business philosophy. You have great passion, and I know you shared a lot of this already, but what really drives you and gives you your motivation to get out of bed in the morning and help the clients that you're helping?

Don Johanson: Typically, many of our new clients find us through our existing happy clients, and they're hearing the wonderful things that they say about our company and the work we do. So, when you have these people who are extremely happy with how they've been treated, how their projects turned out and met their time frames, it makes it easy to get out of bed in the morning. Again, it goes back to those people who appreciate us. I guess life is pretty simple if you look at it. It's really about appreciation; if you appreciate the people that work for you, they appreciate you. If you appreciate your clients, they appreciate you. It just goes hand in hand when I see the appreciation back from the clients, whether they make comments or remarks online, in an e-mail or on a phone call. That's what drives me because it's not necessarily about the painting. It's about people being happy and knowing their needs were met and that they can smoothly move on with their life.

It's also knowing the project is not going to be a struggle for them; it's going to be easy. I always tell people, "Don't sweat the decorating. That part should be fun!" Whether you're remodeling or painting, it should be fun. I tell my clients "Don't stress out. If you have a problem with colors, come to us and we'll help you, or we can give you advice, or we'll send you somewhere, so you can get it right. However, please don't make it a stressful thing, because it should be fun." Creating happy clients with happy workers makes me happy! That pretty much sums it up.

That's great passion! It's undeniable your clients appreciate you helping them and all that passion you bring to the table. You said people sweat the small stuff... what would you say is one of the most significant problems you see clients having when they're trying to get their home or their business painted?

Don Johanson: Well, what I see many times is people collect a lot of stuff through time. Whether it's at home or the office, there's a lot of clutter. And whether those things are important to them, they still stress the fact because they think they have to put together some type of organization plan to empty the space. They make a lot of these projects much more stressful because they're more concerned about stuff than how their painting or decorating project is going to impact their time, their life and everything else. I tell folks "don't make it a big deal. We can move what we need to move. We can help you out with whatever it is; please don't make it a big deal. And most importantly, don't make it a strict timeline." That's the best advice I can give to people who are getting ready for a painting or decorating project; Don't make it a strict time frame because what you're doing is, ultimately, you're undermining the project. "Speed it up, hurry. It's got to get done," etc. and all it does is create stress. Put a realistic time frame together. Enjoy the process. Pick out your colors; figure out the areas and whatever remodeling you want to do, and go step-by-step and don't be in a rush. As soon as you've got everything together, everything comes together very quickly. So, there's no point in rushing your organization for the project.

Would you describe a situation that you had recently with a client who was going through that, where you helped them to turn their thinking around on how they were so stressed out about their project?

Don Johanson: There was an elderly couple, and they were going to be moving. I don't know if it was a downsizing situation, or moving into a condominium or if they are going into a nursing home or a health care facility, they just had a house, and they needed to sell it. They only needed a few pieces of their furniture, and they didn't need all their stuff, and they were absolutely sweating it. They didn't know how to go about it. So, they came to us and we actually referred them to somebody who we work with that went in and helped them with the move, de-clutter and set up an estate sale. They helped them market the house. Told them how to decorate the home so it would sell quickly and helped them with all of those things. This elderly couple wasn't able to put it in perspective, but somebody else was able to help put it in perspective for them and then it was a straightforward project. We figured out what we needed to do to make her home saleable so that they could move. They had their move and their home ready for sale, and they didn't have to worry about moving and de-cluttering and selling or giving things away.

Because what happens is our homes become a massive collection of stuff from our lives. When we get to the tail end of our lives, it's like what do we do with all this stuff? It gets very overwhelming for a lot of folks.

Not only did you create a seamless project for them with the painting, but you found services that actually helped them to de-stress and make the project as smooth sailing as possible. That's fantastic. So, what would be the first thing that someone should do if they're ready to improve their lives, whether it's painting their home, painting their office, painting their business? How do they get started with this stress-free process?

Don Johanson: Well I think the first thing is to figure out exactly what they would like to do and how that would improve their life. Then secondly, they should sit down and figure out what type of budget they have for it. It's much easier to formulate a project around a budget, than a budget around a project, because what happens is things fall through the cracks and then the budget is never really what the budget is. So, if you put together a certain amount of money or time or whatever it may be for that project, then you work around that because those are the known variables. If they do that, then they can call us, and we can put together a good plan; whether it's remodeling or whether it's painting. We'll guide them with the plan and figure out what they want to do with it. They can look through the web or get good pictures from some magazines and come up with some colors and some ideas. Then we can figure out where they're at with their budget and put together a project that's a perfect fit for them. So, this way, they're ultimately happy with the entire process.

Because many times people don't put those pieces together before they move forward with the project, and then they don't wind up with the contractors that they necessarily would have chosen because they have a different style of buying. What many people will do is they'll get a couple of prices, and then that's their budget. If they don't speak with the right people in the first place, the budget is going to be unrealistic and that's the problem.

The other problem is many contractors, will feel as though they can't sell a particular project because they feel as though they know what a person's budget is which is just a guess. So, what they'll do is sell them something less than what they need, and maybe that's not what the person was looking for, or the exact opposite will happen which isn't good either.

So, I think it's good to have your own criteria set before you actually talk to contractors and put together a project that's going to really make you happy and not be stressful. At the end of the day, you're going to be very happy. So, my theory is if the client is happy and the workers are happy, and me as the business owner is happy, it's a win win win. So, we always want to make sure that we give them the end result that they're looking for.

So, to sum it up, who is Don Johanson?

Don Johanson: Who I am... Straightforward, no BS kind of guy who likes to be positive and be around and serve like-minded people with a constant strive to make things simpler and more enjoyable. No stress! Life is here to enjoy not struggle through! The business culture I have created includes a high level of communication via electronics so questions can be answered almost immediately, and issues get resolved before they become problems. My Business Philosophy is... Make the reason people buy from us because it makes their life easier. We don't want our clients experience to be an event but a desired result.

Excellent! What's the best way for people to reach you if they need help?

Don Johanson: Probably the best place is the website JohansonPainting.com, or you can give us a call at (847) 577-6900, and we can set up an appointment with one of our team members or myself, and we'll come out and talk with you about what you're looking to do.

About Don Johanson

Don Johanson is the CEO and founder of Johanson Painting and Handyman Services in Mount Prospect Illinois. Not only has his company won the prestigious Best Picks Award eight years in a row with over 35 years of experience, Don is a true champion of small business with a unique and winning philosophy. He's also an expert in commercial and residential painting and all the integral trades that coincide with painting projects, creating a seamless experience with his clients. As long-standing members of the Painting and Decorating Contractors of America, who provide up-to-date standards in paint application, techniques, and materials, Don's team has the most informed and skilled painters in the marketplace working in the field. Located in Mt. Prospect, Illinois, some of his significant accounts include National Geographic, The Blues Bar, and Lewis Carpet Floor and Home to name a few. These references can attest to Don's unique business philosophy... "We can make you happy!"

WEBSITE
JohansonPainting.com

EMAIL
Don@johansonpainting.com

PHONE
(847) 577-6900

LOCATION
119 South Emerson Street, Ste. 252
Mount Prospect IL 60056

FACEBOOK
Facebook.com/JohansonPainting